HARK! THE HERALD ANGELS SING

FELIX MENDELSSOHN
Arranged by FRED BOCK

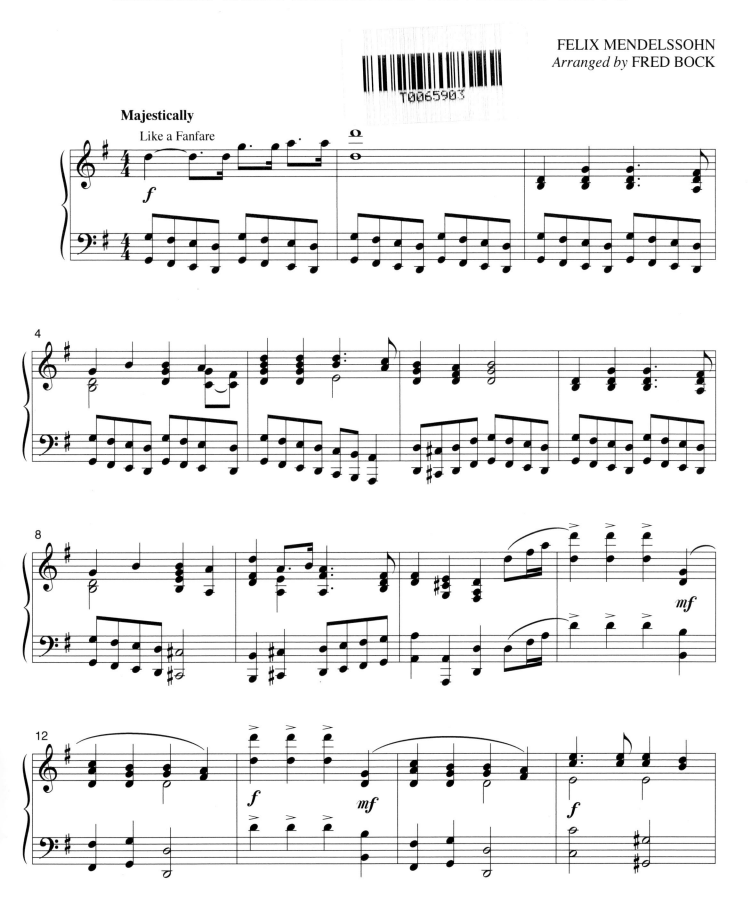

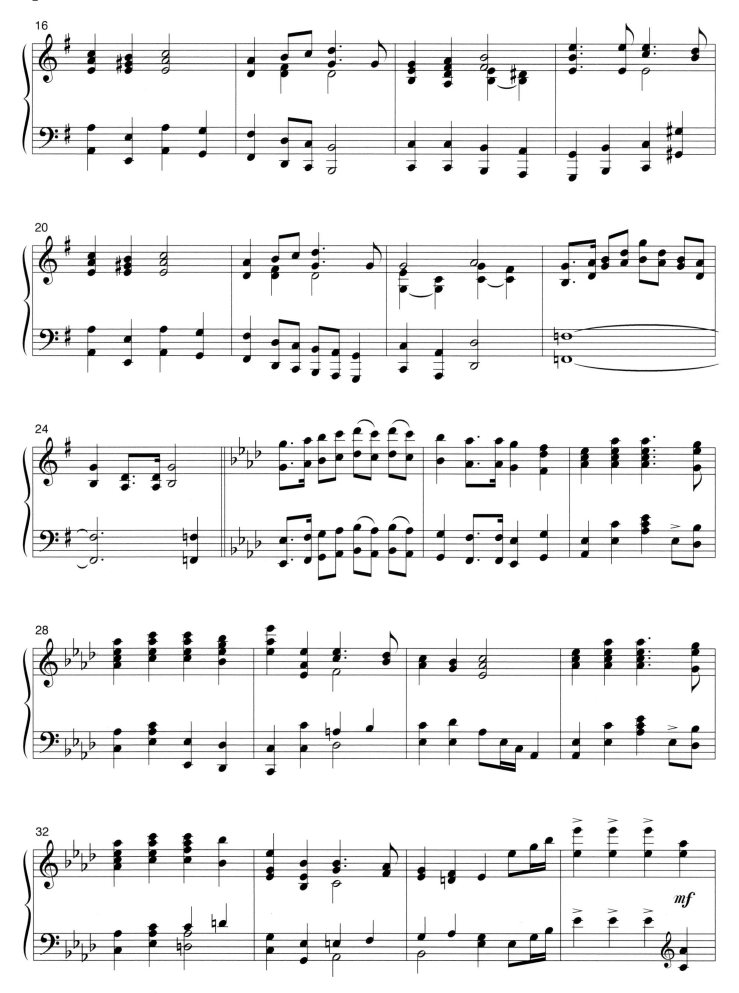

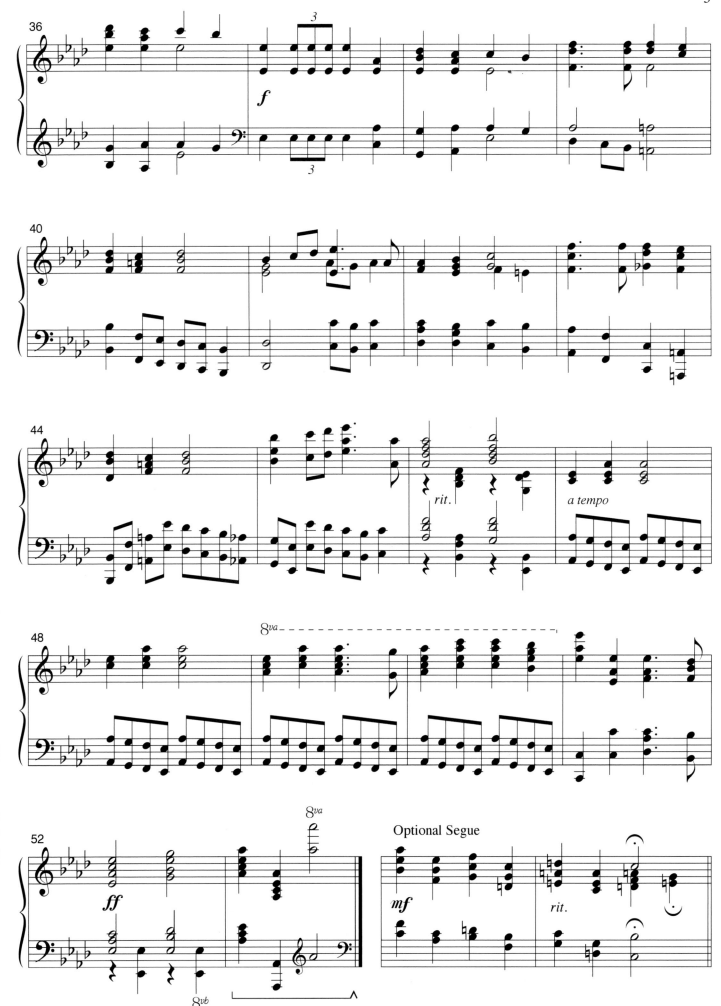

IT CAME UPON THE MIDNIGHT CLEAR

RICHARD S. WILLIS
Arranged by FRED BOCK

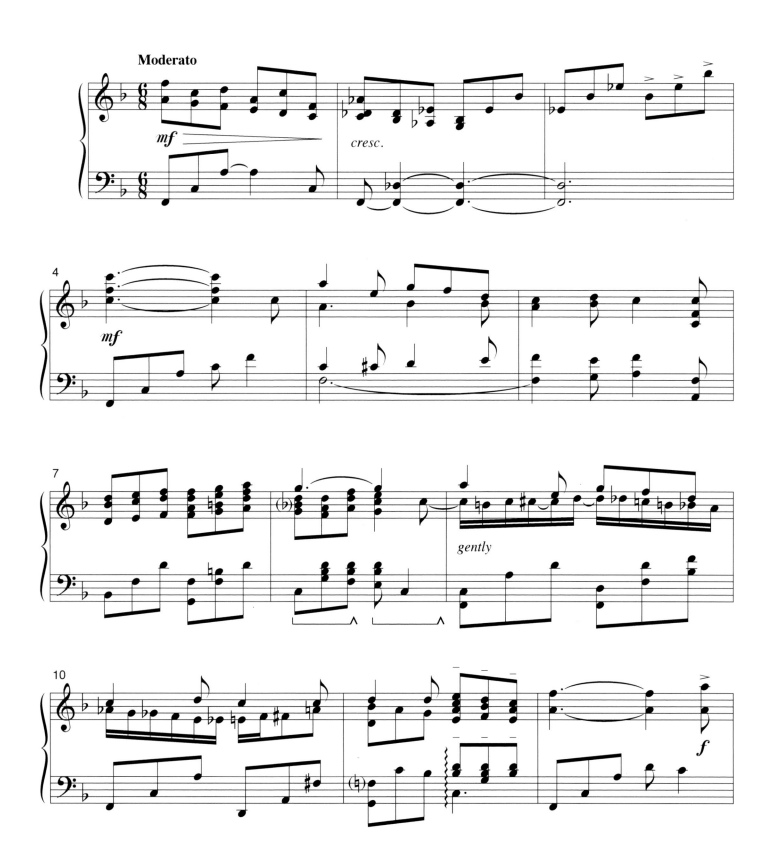

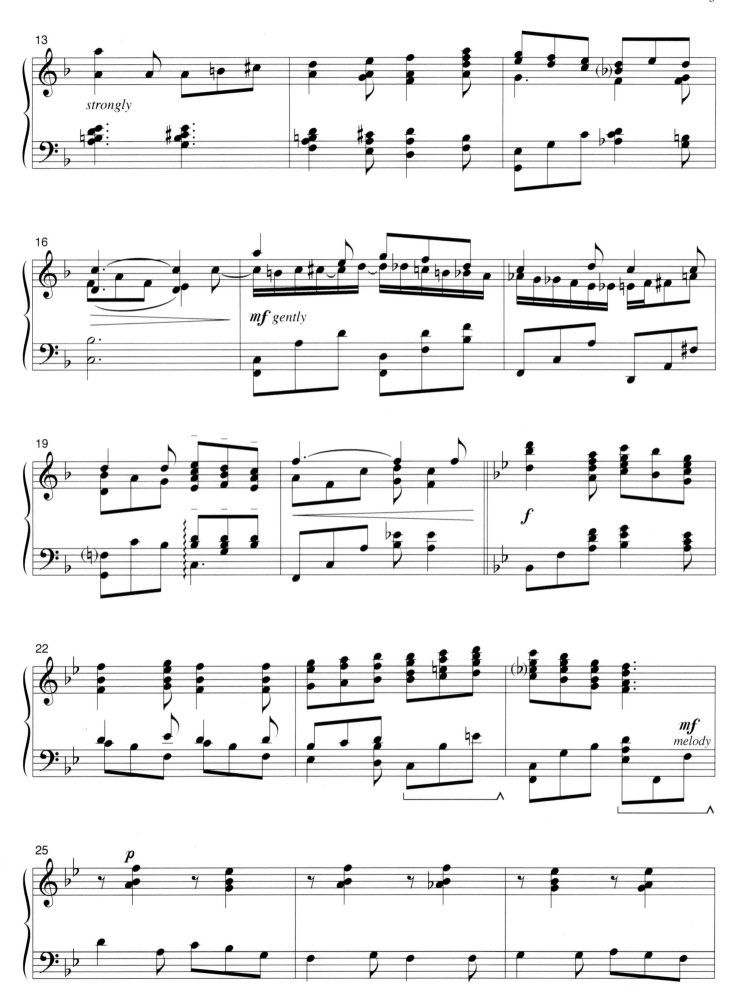

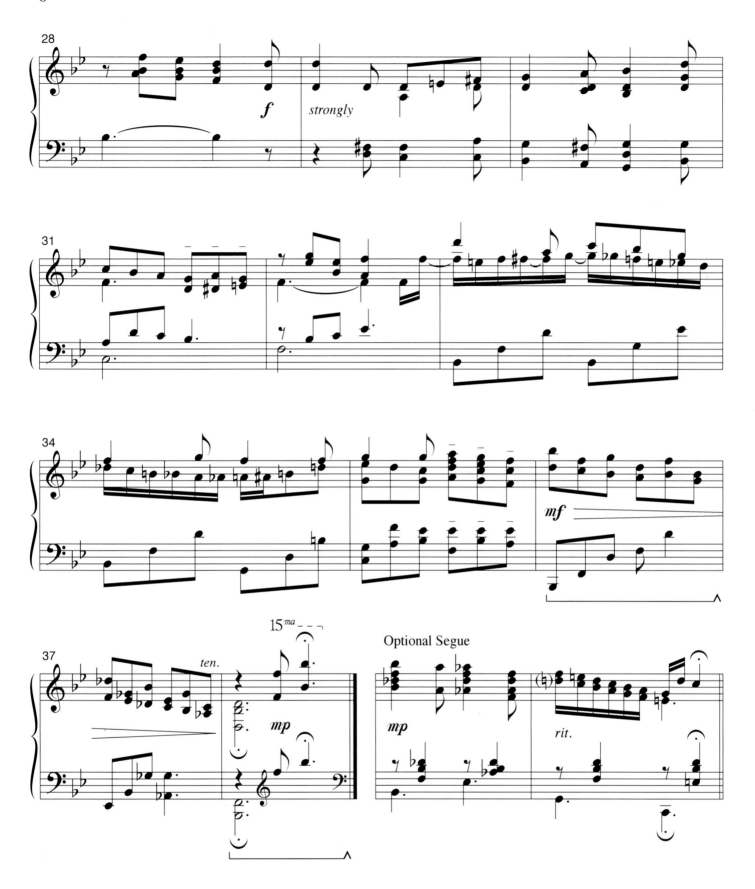

O LITTLE TOWN OF BETHLEHEM

LEWIS H. REDNER
Arranged by FRED BOCK

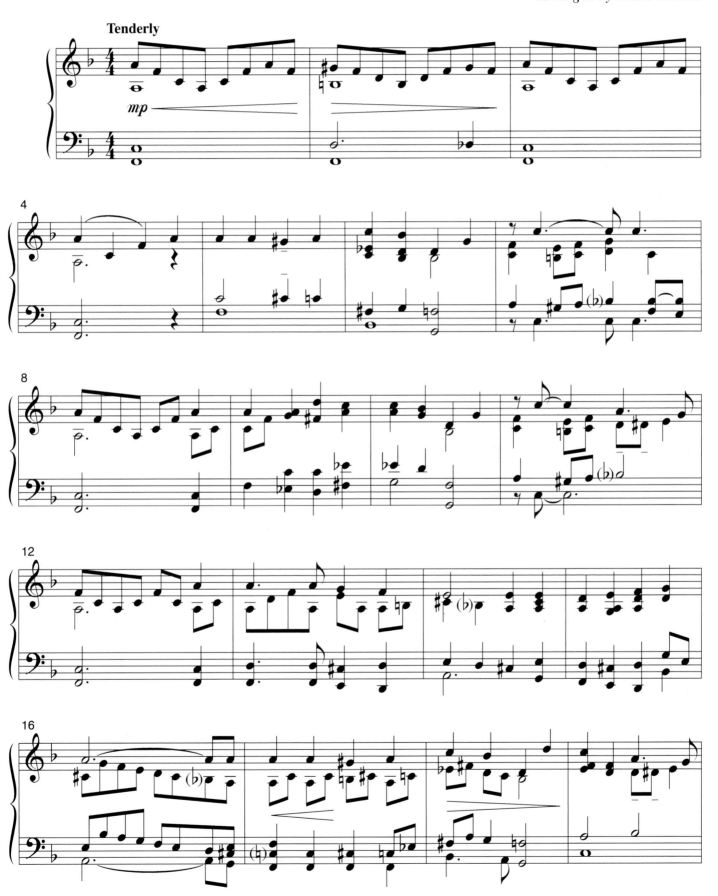

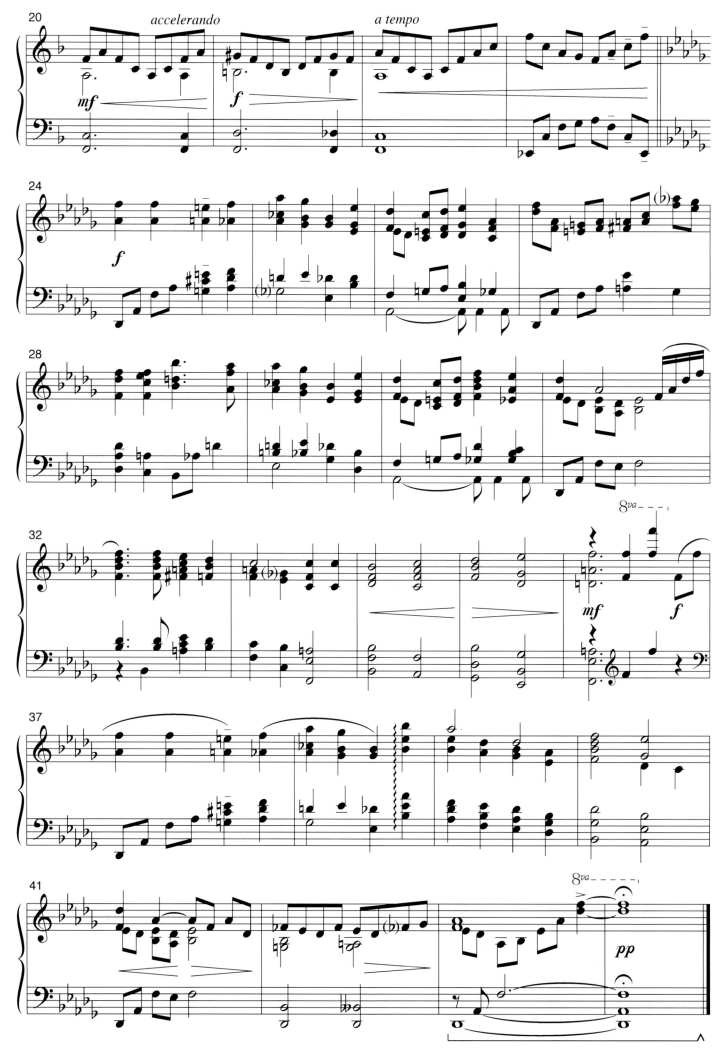